ALSO BY MONICA ANDERSON

Chemistry with Kismet:
Journeying into the Self to Heal the Mind

And What If . . .

CONCEPTS CHALLENGING THE NORM

BY

MONICA ANDERSON

Independently Published
By
Monica Anderson: The Kismet Chemist

This is a work of nonfiction. All names have either been changed
or included with the express permissions of the peoples named.
The events while being true, are that of the perception of the
author and do not reflect those of the characters and people in
the book. All concepts and ideas presented here are the sole
opinion of the author and do not reflect medical or legal advice.
Poem *Whatif* is copyrighted solely by Shel Silverstein, as seen in
A Light in the Attic, published in 1981 by Harper & Row.

First Hardcover edition June 2021

First paperback edition June 2021

Book design by Monica Anderson
Cover Art by Adobe InDesign Stock Photos

ISBN 978-1-7374626-0-6 (hardcover)
978-1-7374626-2-0 (paperback)
978-1-7374626-1-3 (ebook)

https://www.thekismetchemist.com

This book is dedicated to my husband and my children for being my inspirations, my constants, and the purveyors of all things love in my life.

Contents

Prologue

The Little Liar in our Heads

1

What if you could say, "No," without qualifying it?

2

What if you could ask others for help and let them help you?

3

What if you could chase your dreams?

4

What if you could walk through life without being hounded by the Insecurity Fairy?

5

What if you could talk to and not at your children?

6

What if you could listen without judgement to your children?

7

What if you could go back to school, learn to dance, sing at the top of your lungs, take up macrame?

8

What if you could still your mind and body in order to meditate?

9

What if you could accept love to the depth you give it?

10

What if you could walk away from toxicity and never look back?

11

What if you could stand in your own power and declare yourself to the world?

12

What if you could go back to high school and live those days all over again?

13

What if you could eat that piece of cake without feeling guilty?

14
What if you could say, "I love you," hear it back, and trust in it being mutual?

15
What if you could change your life to exactly how you envision it?

Epilogue
You Can, You Are, You Will

Whatif

By: Shel Silverstein

Last night, while I lay thinking here,
some Whatifs crawled inside my ear
and pranced and partied all night long
and sang their same old Whatif song:
Whatif I'm dumb in school?
Whatif they've closed the swimming pool?
Whatif I get beat up?
Whatif there's poison in my cup?
Whatif I start to cry?
Whatif I get sick and die?
Whatif I flunk that test?
Whatif green hair grows on my chest?
Whatif nobody likes me?
Whatif a bolt of lightning strikes me?
Whatif I don't grow taller?
Whatif my head starts getting smaller?
Whatif the fish won't bite?
Whatif the wind tears up my kite?
Whatif they start a war?
Whatif my parents get divorced?
Whatif the bus is late?
Whatif my teeth don't grow in straight?
Whatif I tear my pants?
Whatif I never learn to dance?
Everything seems well, and then
the nighttime Whatifs strike again!

Prologue
The Little Liar in Our Heads

Have you ever found yourself asking question after question, silently inside your head? Going round and round your own mind about the little injustices you perceive to be in the world, or even cursing the great unknown higher power for allowing the rules and limitations of the world to be what they are? Don't worry. You are not alone. I do this all the time.

I have had many conversations with friends and family, even complete strangers, lately and a theme arose. What ifs are running rampant through our minds and through society. It's as though we are all perpetually stuck in the state of the child from the Shel Silverstein poem, *Whatifs*. If you aren't familiar with the poem, you can find it in his poetry book, *A Light in the Attic*. Essentially the poem talks about a child who goes to bed and every night, upon lying his or her head down on the pillow, little Whatifs come dancing through his or her head. The entirety of the poem contains such foolish wonderments, what if the world ends, what if there is a pop quiz I am not prepared for, what if I accidentally go to school in only my underwear. These are not direct references, but you get the picture.

Despite the way the poem comes off as quite foolish and childish, it doesn't change the fact that we, as adults, still engage in the same activity, only now we call it "parental worry" and anxiety. Ah, anxiety, the biggest buzzword of the 21st century. The damnable, overwhelming mindset and thought processes we endure, often silently, until one day we break. That breakage, in actuality is us finding a form of freedom. You find yourself at a place in which you cannot keep holding this thought form inside anymore, you cannot keep hearing the negativity swirl around and around your mind, crippling you with inaction and low self-esteem.

Congratulations! You just took the first step into truly facing these thoughts and emotions, and seeing them for what they truly are: BIG FAT LIES. I tell my kids all the time, as they all unfortunately are miniature versions of who I once walked through life embodying, and I am telling you the same thing right here, right now: Your anxiety lies to you. It is the proverbial serpent in the garden, slithering in, whispering falsehoods in your ears, telling you all the things you think are true, with no basis for the statements made.

Perpetuated perhaps by another person's treatment of you, their words flung at you like the arrow flying from an archer's bow, lodging itself in your mind, and convincing you it was straight to your heart. Sometimes we even conjure it as though working black magic upon ourselves, swirling life experiences, perspectives, and comparisons with other people into a swirling hurricane, leaving destruction in its path.

Does any of this sound like I am crazy for congratulating you? Gosh, I truly hope not. Even if it does, I am standing firm with it, I am proud of you. If you are feeling broken down by your own mind, recognizing something has to give, seeing the fact you cannot continue to move forward in the same old, same old, way you have been, then you are further into healing than you think.

A person suffering from addictions knows the first step to overcoming is to acknowledge the problem. Clearly see the addiction. Seeing, acknowledging, and taking it in as your truth kick starts the healing process. Now you know.

Now you see. Now you can make a concerted effort to make the changes you need to grow, adjust, and become a better version of yourself.

Anxiety is very similar to suffering from an addiction. Your mind becomes addicted to a certain way of thinking about yourself and others, a certain way of perceiving the world. This is not your fault, it truly isn't. In the most egotistical ways, we are all subject to thinking about ourselves, what others have done and said to us, and what the implications of those things have upon our "identity." We see ourselves through the lens of who other people tell us we are, or through our experiences that challenge the magical thinking we had as children. The world and our own ego-centric mindsets have served now to train us to stop believing in the impossible. Replaced instead with bills, worries, and whatifs.

After undergoing many changes and upheavals in life, I found myself in an anxiety state-of-mind continually. Wondering perpetually why things had to be how they were, why certain people were unable or unwilling to change who they are, and why it seemed as though no one else saw the world the way I do. It was a form of perpetual self-torture.

Too often I found myself wondering, *what is wrong with me?* It took many hard times, many events which crumbled the foundations of everything I had built, and losing people in my life over and over again until I finally stopped wondering and started looking at the whole of my life. Seeing the broader view of everything that happened, I was able to see new perspectives I was unable to prior. Spoiler alert: there is nothing wrong with me. Double spoiler alert: there is nothing wrong with you either.

There is no point in beating yourself up over what has happened, who has said what, or the whys of situations in life. Those questions, while common, understandable, and a natural human reaction, are not serving a purpose for you. When the answers are meant to come to you, they will. The Universe has a way of bringing forth exactly what you need to know, exactly when you need to know it. You being here, reading this, looking for answers, all of it means only one thing: it is time for you to see another side of common questions, so you are able to finally let them go and move forward.

1

What if you could say, "No," without qualifying it?

Are you a classic "people pleaser"? I certainly am. I worry myself into circles all the time about if my answer to this person or that person is something viewed as acceptable, if they are going to be upset with me, if I am doing something I shouldn't. Worst of all is the perpetual Mom-guilt. Mom-guilt is the absolute worst.

As a mother I never want to let my children down, I never want to do or say something which is going to hurt them or prevent them from living their life to the fullest.

Of course this is taken to a completely unreasonable level. When they ask to stay out an extra hour despite it being a school night, I have had to literally train myself, courtesy of my husband, David's, insistence I am not a terrible mother, to say, "No."

When I began learning how to say no to another person, I was perpetually caught up in the qualifying state-of-mind. Asked to go out to dinner with friends, I would respond with, "I'm really sorry, but . . ." followed by a long run-on sentence filled with excuses and explanations. I felt the need to do this because I am a hardcore people pleaser. I don't want to let anyone else down. I would rather let myself down than another person. I lived this way for years, until it became a painful hindrance to me living my life fully.

I wanted to be a hermit. I wanted to take time out for myself. To tell my friends or family who would ask me for this favor or that favor,

"Nope. I am taking a bath and reading a book tonight. Completely booked, check again later this week," and leave it at that. Ah, the joys of being able to simply say no and then live your life knowing it isn't going to change the love others have for you.

More people than otherwise, struggle daily with the sense of a need to qualify when they answer someone else in a way perceived as negative. I am challenging you today to change your perception. Saying no does not have to be a negative thing. It is a positive, self-affirming response when it comes from the heart. You are allowed to say no. You don't even have to tell someone what else you have planned, just saying no, trusting the response will be one to affirm your choice.

Why would you trust that? Because you get back what you put out. You really do. Sometimes it seems as though you don't. Believe me, I get that. I know there are a million examples I could give in which I have put this out into the Universe, or that out there, and the response I received was less than ideal. The reason is not because the Universe seeks to smack us down and put us into our place, but because in our heart of hearts, it was not what we were actually exuding.

Self-assurance comes from self-love. To be confident and sure of who you are, what you deserve, and how others will respond, you have to first love yourself completely. I am not going to lie to you and tell you it is going to be an easy journey. I will promise you, however, at the end of the journey you will find nothing but joy, abundance, and all the things you have sent out in positivity and hope in the world. If you are sitting here reading this, wondering to yourself, what do I know about your life, what do I know about what struggles you have experienced. I understand your feelings.

I do not know what you have suffered, but I do know suffering. I do not know how hard you have had it, but I do know hardship. I also am intimately familiar with deep self-loathing internally while being a ray of love and light for others outwardly. I know, in order to get what you give; you must first give it to yourself. That is why I am here to tell you all of these things. So you can discover what I did: saying no, standing in your truth and power, and loving yourself is the ultimate rewarding experience.

Everyone has the ability to do what they want, when they want, and how they want (at least to some extent). Think of a homeless person, they do not live under the weight of a mortgage. They do not have life easy, but they still don't have to worry about slaving their life away for another person in order to pay for a seeming status symbol. Bad example? Perhaps, or you could see them in a completely different light. I see people who come into my provincial town every summer, they are nomads, moving from place to place as the weather and their own souls permit them to. People always see them as vagrants, but I have grown to see them as free. They move when they want, stay when they want, live how they want, and make no excuses nor apologies for how they make their way in the world. What heroic means of living life, truly.

My challenge for you:

1. **SAY NO.** Do not qualify it, do not feel guilty. Say no and then go about your life exactly as you would have if you had not been asked about or to do something you did not want or plan on.

2. **ASK YOURSELF WHY.** Why do you feel as though you need to justify your actions? Why do you feel as though you are unable to respond to requests without qualifications?

3. **EXPERIENCE LIFE ON YOUR OWN TERMS.** Arguably one of the more challenging ones to do, I want you to spend an entire week experiencing life only on your own terms. Answer to no one but yourself. Make decisions which are solely based upon what you feel in your heart. Follow your inner guidance system and live for you and your own happiness.

2

What if you could ask for help, and allow others to help you?

I am headstrong, stubborn, and have more often than not faced down life on my own terms, doing it my way. This is mostly because I have been afraid to ask another person for help. Why? Because I *hate* feeling as though I am burdening another person with the things I want to do or choose to do in my life. The perpetual feeling of being a burden is truly one of the most complicated parts of my psyche I have ever had to overcome.

One of the things that drives my husband, David, completely bonkers is when I talk about how I don't want to ask for help because I don't want to be a burden on him and on anyone else. This feeling was drilled into me over the course of many years I spent with my ex-husband. My illnesses were thrown in my face as being a problem, a burden. If I was not able to clean the house, make supper, keep the kids out of his hair, and deliver in the bedroom when it was expected, there were a multitude of colorful insults slung at me. Worthless, lazy, fat, pathetic, a terrible mother, an unwanted wife, and above all such a heavy burden. My physical health was what made me the biggest burden to him.

It took me more than five years after the divorce to stop apologizing for being sick. Even something small like a cold, and I would push myself to make sure everything would get done around the house that needed to get done, and I would apologize incessantly. I loathed asking anyone to do anything, and because I used to be a bit of a control freak when it came to cleanliness, again because of the standards that my ex demanded of me, when I would ask for help and get it, I wasn't able to truly appreciate it. I would go and reclean what was already cleaned.

This became a toxic cycle. I couldn't ask for help and when I would attempt it, the help I got wasn't what I was hoping for and then I would get angry. Angry with both the person who was just trying to help me, but also angry with myself. It is incredibly difficult to find appreciation when you are constantly caught up in whether you are being burdensome when asking for help. It is even more difficult when you ask for help with an unreasonable expectation of the person performing to your standards. This kind of challenge and inner struggle is something that requires recognition, and overcoming.

One major thing, if you are anything like me, is you have to realize, if you are the kind of person who is always there for another person as soon as they ask you for help, that person is also there for you. Asking for help does not mean you are incapable. It does not mean you are a burden. It doesn't make you weak, or pathetic, or sad. It makes you STRONG. It means you recognize when you aren't able to complete something on your own, and you know someone else is capable of collaborating on it with you.

We live in a world that has become far too self-serving and the focus has been taken off of community, kinship, and generosity. It creates the environment of "every man or woman for himself or herself." With this mentality, there is an unbalanced sense of giving and taking. Much of the spiritual community will tell you, we are being called to step more fully into our divine feminine nature, to have an equal and even energy exchange in all that we do, and to learn to properly blend the masculine and feminine aspects within all of us into harmony.

Every person approaches that which we are being tasked now to do, in a different way. For me, it is all about learning boundaries, limitations, and asking for help. Seeing just where it is, I am unable to complete something for myself, and trusting in the fact there are others in the world, and in my close circle, have the skills to help me and teach me. Asking for help is not always the easiest thing to do.

When you are dealing with a lifetime's worth of trust issues, asking for help can become something of a phobia. *Am I going to be betrayed? Will this person share the things I share with them with the world? Will I be punished once more for trusting someone?*

All those tormented mindsets needed to be changed, because I needed to learn how to ask for help. I needed to learn how to allow others to show me that trust is possible, getting help is possible, being loved is possible, and above all, being supported by others is possible. It was not a lesson in life I took lightly, but one which involved breaking myself down piece by piece, viewing all the different situations I had survived, lived through, and come out the other side stronger because of.

Much of the lessons I learned in this whatif came directly from writing my first book *Chemistry with Kismet: Journeying into the Self to Heal the Mind*. While writing *Chemistry*, I had to trust others to read the imperfect versions, to see the things I could not see for myself, and to help me to perfect and polish it to the best of my abilities. Much of it was done solo, or with the help of family and friends. I couldn't afford a publishing firm, I couldn't garner the attention I desired from agents, and I couldn't pay for an editor who would have charged more than my family could spare.

These facts led to the imperfect copies of the books, hitting circulation in the first wave. The funniest part of the fact that the first books purchased were what I like to call the "Whoops, Special Collector's Edition," is when I announced on my personal page and my author platforms about the copy containing printing errors, there was a mad rush of people who wanted the "Special" copy. Not because it was a mistake, but because of a firm faith in my friends and family that my writing, my books, would take me higher and farther in my life than I could fathom. They wanted to help me get there.

You likely have people all around you, people you tend to discount because you are discounting yourself. People who want to help you, not hurt you, because they love you. You likely have someone, even just one, would drop everything and be there for you if you would just *ask*. Asking for help is one beautiful way to open the doors of your heart to see the love others have for you in this world.

My challenge for you:

1. **ASK FOR HELP ONCE A WEEK.** Ask for help with something you have a tendency to do for yourself. Whether that be dishes, laundry, going to the store, or even something larger like help on a project you have been working on diligently. Ask for help once a week for a month, allowing another person to fully commit and help you, trusting they are there for you.

2. **DO A REVIEW.** Review times in which you have asked for help and received it. How did you feel? How did it make your life easier? Did it make your life harder? What about the situation made it either easier or harder? Write it down, make a bullet point list, or write it in a journal. When you are done writing it down, go back and read it. How do you feel about it now? Do you feel connected to the situation still? Why or why not? Breaking

things down like this will give you the opportunity to get those harder moments out, out of your mind, out of your heart, and you now can heal from it and leave it where it truly belongs, in the past.

3. **HELP SOMEONE ELSE.** It is time to flip the script. You can be the change that you want to see in the world by willingly setting the example of helping another person out of the kindness of your heart. Go on your social media and see someone who is having a hard time. Whatever the situation they are dealing with, ask yourself, *what can I do to make this lighter for him/her? How can I show him/her there are people he/she doesn't realize here to help?* Be the person for someone else that you would want to have someone be for you. This is one beautiful way to establish that first part of an energy exchange. It may not always come

back to you in the same way, but if you do this, the person you have gifted with your help then pays it forward, you have now created a ripple effect of love and kindness in the world. You have now changed the world for the better. Nothing and no one can take something that incredible from you.

3

What if you could chase your dreams?

I have dreamt much of my life of sitting down and writing the next great American novel. I was going to be the next J.K. Rowling, the next Harper Lee. I was going to write a book or a series that would take the world by storm, change lives, and everyone would love my stories. This still is my dream, though perhaps not in the fictional world anymore, now I want my words, my thoughts, my perspectives, and my life experiences to be a beacon of light for other people struggling in life. I want, desire, dream of changing a life by telling of my darkness, using the once perceived "differently wired" nature of my thinking brain to help someone feel less alone in the world.

In order to see this dream really truly be made manifest, I had to chase it. I had to sit my stubborn tooshie down at a computer, or with a pen and paper, and do the thing that I wanted to be known for: WRITE. Gah! What a serious challenge it was in the very beginning. I said for years, "Someday I am going to write a book about my life." In my heart of hearts, I never believed I was capable of it. Sure, I had tried to write this book, that book, this blog, and so on and so forth. You get the picture, I am sure.

Dreams are not meant to remain in the night, behind closed eyes, and in a sense of fantasy and unattainability. What I have learned, what I am here to tell you, right now, is your dreams want you to live them as much, if not more, than you want them to be real. Dreams are not simply fantasy moments designed to escape from the humdrum of real life. They are there to show you what you are capable of, what you are meant to do and be in this life, and give you inspiration to start journeying forward.

There were a million and a half reasons for me to never chase my dream of being a published author. I wrote my first book, and this book, on a laptop that has far since lived beyond its prime, a secondhand gift from my husband, and one that has crashed more times than I can count when I attempted to use it as a work-from-home hub. By all accounts, my books are perpetually at risk of simply disappearing because of a technological crash. That is just one.

For years I kept up the premise that I hated to write on a computer. I needed to write longhand before I could consider writing a book on a computer. Then I would begin writing in notebooks and journals and I didn't want to transcribe it because it was just *so much work*. One excuse after another, after another. And that was quite literally exactly what they were, excuses.

I was too fearful of the potentials of failure and the potentials of success to really take the first step into making my dreams a reality. Fear of failure and fear of success while seemingly oxymoronic to have simultaneously, I see more like the saying, "there's a thin line between love and hate." They are two sides of the same coin. Heads and you are going to live your life being afraid of failing everything that you attempt, and tails, you are going to live your life fearing finding the success you dream about.

Why would someone fear success? How could it hold you back? Don't worry, I do see how illogical it seems, but allow me to shift your perspectives on this. I am a person who has experienced karma in many facets. I know what generational karma looks and feels like, the struggle and journey required to break free of it. I also have seen first-hand the presentation of ancestral karma in my life, how to stop the cycles, and change the storyline for myself and for my children. Finding success truly comes with its own set of possibilities involving change and transition and public recognition. I do not honestly know anyone who would want to stand up in front of a crowd of people, opening themselves up for the public to take pot-shots at them. Then there is the inner insecurity that comes to the surface, asking, *What right do you have to stand in your power?*

Asking why someone would fear failure, well, to be honest I think this is something we all fully understand. Crippling each one of us with indecision and inaction, how could anyone ever deem themselves worthy to chase their dreams if all that will result is a big, fat FAIL?! This was one manner of living my life that kept me from doing just that, living my life. Dreams? Dreams were relegated to the things I would envision and follow up with telling myself how unworthy I was to even attempt.

I do not want you to endure one more moment of thinking you are unworthy, living in fear, or holding yourself back continually. What do you dream of doing or being? Why are you holding yourself back?

Everyone has to start somewhere. You only need to start with permission. Give yourself permission to dream. Give yourself permission to chase your dreams. Even though I stand firm in the statement, you do not need permission from another person to chase your dreams, I am sitting here today telling you: CHASE YOUR DREAMS.

Do not live your life holding yourself back. Fears are meant to be acknowledged and overcome; they are not meant to overcome you. *Easier said than done, Monica.* Yes, I know. I know how easy it is for me to sit here, write these pretty words on paper, but I beseech you to take into consideration the opening of this chapter. My dream is literally me sitting here, writing these words down with the full intention of them reaching you, taking hold, and changing your mindset, so you can change your life.

I am not allowing my fears to hold me back. I will stand bastion from you against the encroaching darkness of your own fears, so you too can live the life, live the dreams, you are meant to.

My challenge for you:

1. **DREAM BIGGER.** What is it that you have dreamt of since your childhood? What is it that you have dreamt of in your early adulthood years? What dreams have

you put on a shelf in your mind under the title "Not Possible," or "Illogical"? Dust those dreams off, now dream even bigger than them.

2. **TAKE THE FIRST STEP.** Say you want to be a writer, or an artist, or a musician, okay, now you know what you want to be or do, it is time to think about what you need to create the reality of it in your life. If you want to be a writer, get a piece of paper and a pen and write. It doesn't matter if it is something that you deem as "good," it matters only that you have taken the first step forward. If you want to be an artist, what is the medium you want to use? Go get the supplies. You do not need to break the bank, you just need to start small, practice, and work your way forward. If you want to be a musician, what instrument do you want to play? Do you want to sing? What do you need to

start that? Taking the first step brings about empowerment, quick, fast, and in a hurry. In a world driven by instant gratification, this is the best step you can do, the very first.

3. **STOP ASPIRING AND START BEING.** Early in 2021, I was emailing authors and musicians about including their words and/or lyrics in my first book, *Chemistry with Kismet*, and I received the best advice through an emailed response from Brian McDonald. After telling me he simply did not have free time to read and review my book, I told him I completely understood. Then, when I felt as though the conversation had been what it was meant to be, I received another email from him: "One more thing. Try not to call yourself an "aspiring" writer or author. If you write you are a writer. You mean that you'd like to be published – that's

different. You cannot give ANYONE the power to bestow the title "writer" or "author" upon you. You are giving others too much power. You decide, not them. You are a writer. No one else will believe it until you do." That advice, those words, changed my perspective, changed my life. I am an author. I do not aspire to that which I already know I am, I simply am. So stop "aspiring" to do or be something, and just simply be that. You are not an aspiring artist; you are an artist. Just as I was told, I am telling you, no one has the power to deem you worthy, you have to know your own worth and stand tall in that.

4

What if you could walk through life without being hounded by the Insecurity Fairy?

I love the Fae, the Tuatha De Danann, the blessed fairies running around the world, making magic a tangible force in the world. I love the tales and the mythology of the race found in the annals of Irish/Celtic history. What I don't love is the Insecurity Fairy. That mythical force buzzing around inside your head when you are standing in front of the mirror, doing your makeup, while getting ready for a hot date, telling you, "Is that really how you are going to do your hair? Don't you think you should wear it up, or down? What about curling it? What if it doesn't curl right? Maybe you should cancel."

The Insecurity Fairy isn't actually a fairy, it is a small buzzing voice inside our heads, trained to believe we are not good enough, thin enough, pretty enough, handsome enough, just all around not enough. Self-love is a wonderful way to combat the insecurity fairy. To stand firm in who we are and say, "No more! I am beautiful! I am handsome! I am smart! I am worthy! I am enough!"

Yet standing up to the buzzing requires us to don our battle armor and prepare ourselves for an inner war that leaves behind blood, sweat, and tears. It is meant to be this way. It is meant to be a battle of wills, to the death, where we strip the fairy of its illusory wings and leave it buried six feet under. Limping our way off the battlefield, and taking all the time our hearts require to heal.

Perhaps I am painting too brutal of an image of what this is truly like, but when I went to war with my own Insecurity Fairy, I made sure that I was armed to the hilt with every positive thought and statement anyone had ever made toward me. I knew, inherently, I would be facing down the deepest pains and darknesses, and staring them in the face to tell them: YOU ARE WRONG! I AM ENOUGH! I AM WORTHY! I AM BEAUTIFUL! GO BACK TO THE HELLISH PLACE YOU CAME FROM!

As though I were Gandalf standing on the bridge in Moria, screaming, "You shall not pass!" I went toe to toe with the monsters that I had dubbed Insecurity Fairies. Cause guys, I had about twenty of them buzzing around my head, telling me each and every flaw in my skin, face, hair, body, personality, thought process, and life. All the things I was doing wrong, all the things I was failing, all the people I was letting down. It was the worst of the worst battles. But I won!

You have your own battle armor, your own means of going to war with the Insecurity Fairy, unfairly buzzing fallacies of who you are through your mind, crippling you with indecision and self-doubt. Go to war! Do what you need to do because I am here to tell you: YOU ARE ENOUGH! YOU ARE MORE THAN ENOUGH, YOU ARE LOVED, BLESSED, CHERISHED, AND THIS WORLD NEEDS YOU IN IT!

Much of my insecurities were spawned through my own belief that the thoughts and emotions of another person outweighed those of my own. I placed a much higher premium on the words uttered by the people around me, but only if they were negative words. If anyone would be so wonderful as to tell me I am beautiful, a talented author, a skilled blogger, a loving wife and mother, well, those people simply had to be as crazy as I was believing what the negative thoughts in my head were telling me.

Do you see the problem here? Let me elaborate for you. In order to see myself in the light of truth, to believe in myself, to love myself, I had to let go of caring about anything said to me from another person. I had to spend my time focusing solely upon each negative thought and then seeing what the reality of it was.

Let me use my writing as an example. My first book was, is, an imperfect piece of work. Lacking in proper editing passes, containing far too many "that's" throughout its entirety, and frankly, needing another eighteen or so rounds of editing. So why would I be so bold as to publish it in the state it is? The only answer I have for that question is, *it was time*. There is a saying, publish or perish. Though I don't always agree with it, in this one case, it was a one or the other for me. I knew, in order for me to feel ready to move forward, I had no choice but to publish the damn thing, errors and all.

Finding out that the first round of books contained printing errors, shifted pages, and all around not what I envisioned for the first printed copies to come out looking like, I could have too easily used this to justify NEVER writing again. Screw that, I am not going to be that person, you should never allow yourself to be that person either. I instead fully embraced who I am, what I wrote, and let the "Whoops" be what it was.

Reading Mark Manson's *The Subtle Art of Not Giving A F*ck*, this is one moment in which I can tell you definitively, I chose to not give a f*ck. I chose to not care about whether or not it was exactly perfect, but instead to embrace and love what I had put into the world. I will never claim to be the next great American author, even if I once hoped to be. What I will claim is this, my writing inspires me. It is bravery, daring, and truth wrapped in an imperfect bundle with a glittery bow atop it. My point here is, if I can do it, so can you.

Whatever it is that you want to do in life, who you want to be, even just how you want to see yourself, do it. Screw the buzzing fairy and be who you already know you are. It is that simple.

My challenge for you:

1. **MAKE A LIST.** Yes, be that woman or man. Make a list. List every positive quality you have. Now list every quality you want to have, but don't change the category. List who you are, even if part of the list entails parts you feel you aren't. This will give you an actual, accurate view of *you*.

2. **LEAVE BEHIND THE BUZZ.** What more can you want than to walk through your life without the incessant buzzing of "not good enough" comments going through your head? (Yeah, yeah, yeah a million dollars, penthouse suite, and Lamborghini, we all want that, but let's be a little more realistic here, we are doing

inner work after all.) Spend a day truly replacing the buzz with positive reinforcement as soon as it begins to float in. You start hearing, "Wow, you are so fat." Put a stopper in the mouth of that bedeviled fairy, and combat it with, "These jeans make my butt look phenomenal!" You know what, your butt does look phenomenal, those jeans are a fantastic choice, and you have definitely lost weight. Fat is as much a state of mind as it is something you can change about your body.

3. **GO OUT AND BE YOUR FABULOUS SELF.** Do not live your life on anyone else's terms but yours. Wear what makes you feel sexy, do your hair in the exact way that makes you feel attractive, laugh at the top of your lungs, burp as loud as you can, and just be yourself. Be your fabulous self, fully assured that who you

are is who the world wants to see. No one is judging you, so why are you judging yourself? Stop doing that! I am not judging you; your friends are not judging you, the sexy woman on the subway isn't judging you, the man of your dreams standing on the corner while waiting for the crosswalk light to flash is definitely not judging you. No one is, so why are you? Be yourself. Love yourself.

5

What if you could talk to and not at your children?

I have four children. I have been and still am an imperfect parent. I have learned through my journey as a mother that it is important to listen to your children and talk to them. Talking at them breeds discord and resistance. Do you know what the difference between talking at your children and talking to them? If not, you now know your starting point.

I used to be a mother that did nothing but lecture and talk at my kids. I wouldn't allow a word in edgewise and lived under the guise of "Mother knows best." I was narrowminded, and controlling. Mostly because I was either being controlled by someone else (my ex) or because I had just gotten out of my too controlling first marriage and was still trying to keep things exactly as they were meant to be to appease him. I needed to change my approach to parenting.

Nothing could make that fact more clear to me than when my children began coming home telling me horrifying stories of the things they endured at the hands of their father and stepmother. The way they were showing fear and anxiety simply through talking about what happened there, I knew that something needed to change.

I tried for years to bring to the attention of my ex-husband the things our children would bring up when they would come home. The fear they exhibited, the troublesome behaviors, comments, and attitudes they were showing. Each time I would bring it up, the kids would go back, be punished for talking to me, and come home more traumatized than they were when they left. I stopped being able to try to co-parent in those days. Standing up for my kids, advocating for them, it was hurting them more than helping them. The only thing left to me was open communication within my home.

You see, children have more perceptive natures. They see more, hear more, and feel more than we give them credit. Which inevitably means that it is our job to *see* them, *hear* them, and *allow them to have a voice*. We need to see our children as the next generation of adults, and treat them, raise them, teach them to know about themselves and the world so they go out into it capable. To do this we cannot just talk at them expecting what we say to matter above and beyond every other thing in the world. We have to talk to them.

That too is one of the biggest battles. My girls have a large variety of friend groups, and I operate my house with an "open door" policy. I mean it with the kids, and they know that. Rarely will one of my girls' friends come to the house and knock on the door. They know my home is as much their home as their own homes are. They often take to calling me and David, Mom and Dad, when they are over as well. Hugging me and telling me they love me.

This isn't because I am a better parent than their parents. It is not because I am special. It is because I open my heart, mind, and home to them and allow them to talk about anything and everything. (Granted, I also feed them, which goes a long way, particularly with the teenagers.) I allow for an open forum of conversation topics, while simultaneously talking about my own experiences, insecurities, and the journeys I have undergone to overcome those moments.

To raise our children to break free of the "cancel culture" generation they are in, they need to understand more about the world and truly see what fights we all should be fighting. Talk to your kids. Talk to them about why they think that "cancelling" this or that is what they should throw their hearts and minds behind when there are other issues in the world begging for attention and focus. What is more important, the bravado of lyrics from a scrawny, white, inner-city kid who made it big as a rapper because of his shock quality, or the elephants being poached because of their tusks leading them to the brink of extinction.

When we do not spend the time to talk to the younger generation about what REAL issues in the world look like, they glom on to mainstream media, and the animals facing extinction, the trees being cut down impacting the oxygen levels in our world, the energy sector that could be searching for alternative means to clean up the air quality and work in harmony with mother nature, (and that is just to name a few of the issues our world is facing) get swept under the rug. We are giving them power to determine who is "in" and who is "out" because of the pervasive nature of the "cancel culture" but we are not talking to them about anything of import.

My challenge for you:

1. **TALK TO A CHILD.** Sit down with your child, your friend's child, go to a school, do something. Don't be creepy, obviously, but sit down and ask a child a question about something that matters to them, and listen to what they feel is important about that topic. Just talk to the child. Don't try to assert your opinion and take on any part of what they are talking about, just ask questions, throw in some conversational support, but allow them to dominate the conversation while giving them your undivided attention.

2. **GIVE A CHILD SOMETHING REAL TO CANCEL.** What is the most important thing you can see in the world

needing to be changed? Why is this change important, not only to you, but to everyone? Why does it light a passionate blaze within you to think about the changes and benefit you can see? Now talk to your child about it. Light that fire within them. Show them what it is like to stop focusing on Hollywood, this singer, that singer, and focus more on the world and the things that are begging to be changed.

3. **SHOW YOUR CHILD THE RESPECT YOU ASK FOR.** We all know the "respect your elders," take on the world. We grew up hearing it. Now to spout that off to the younger generation, actually risks us coming off as pompous jackasses. Yes children should respect their elders, but we need to show them how to do so by setting the example. Do you respect the emotions your child discusses with you? If

you don't show their emotions and thoughts a level of respect, how can you genuinely expect them to respect you and your emotions? You have to *teach* them what respect looks like. Not simply demanding it of them without teaching them full understanding of respect.

6

What if you could listen without judgement to your children?

Ah, listening to your child. What a strain this simple action truly could be. I know it, I have kids. I know how they can go on and on about this topic, or that video game. I know the frivolous conversations about what this popular girl said at school, or what the coolest boy in class was acting like in front of everyone. There is an urge, deep within you, to stab your ears with hot pokers, deafening yourself, because the things your kids are focusing on seem so childish.

Guess what, it is childish. It is supposed to seem that way to us. We have bills, a mortgage, a job, a boss that won't listen, coworkers that are ganging up on us, and a spouse that won't do anything around the house without an argument making us feel as though pulling our teeth from our mouths would be more appealing, and we are stressed and anxious and worried. Now we come home, and we have to listen to the most ludicrous topics of conversation with our kids because Sally-says-a-lot told our daughter that her hair color looks store bought, which it was, which is a major inconvenience, and "Why can't we be like the Bloomfield's and get our hair professionally done every two weeks?"

It is enough to drive any mother or father directly to a stiff drink. I get it, I have been there. The thing is, if you hear the things that your child is saying, taking yourself out of the mix, what you will hear instead is what underlying insecurities our children are walking around carrying. They feel these things are important because they are children. We are tasked with listening, not telling them they are being ridiculous. It is our purpose as parents to hear and validate their feelings, and through validation, change the way they view themselves and the situation. This is meant to be done through nonjudgmental thoughts, and unconditional love.

This is what you, and I, signed up for the day we became parents. We signed up for raising a tiny human into a functional member of society knowing that the person we brought into the world would learn the most about the world through our lessons, our love, and the lives that we provide for them. Parenting is not a small thing. It is a very big undertaking. You are responsible for a life. You are responsible for your life and the life of another human being. How you talk to them and listen to them will form the foundational basis of what they think, feel, and believe in themselves. It is our job, our duty, our right, and our honor to DO THIS THE RIGHT WAY for our children.

My theory on parenting is we either learn what to do or what not to do from the lessons of our parents. Did you sit down and talk everything out with your Mom and Dad when you were a teenager? Did they show you that the fleeting passions and interests that you had as a child were as important to them as they were to you? Did you feel as though you were fully embraced by them throughout all the stages of your life? Or did you learn what they failed to do for you and now you have promised yourself, you are going to do it differently?

My mom was not approachable for me when I was in high school. A fact she and I have broken down together time and again. Through my own mentality, and situations in life, I simply did not feel as though I could talk to her about the things occurring in my life. I was terrified of letting her down, of being judged, or being punished by the things happening in my life. Simultaneously I felt as though nothing that was occurring in my life would truly matter to her. How was I supposed to tell her I was being manipulated into having sex? How was I supposed to tell her that I had lost my virginity and teenage freedom? How was I supposed to tell her that everything occurring in my life was spiraling out of control and I didn't know what to do?

This is something we are meant to change. It is something, as an adult with children of my own, I have discussed with my mother at length. We have talked about the way I felt fearful of letting her down, the way I felt as though I wouldn't be heard, and the way I felt as though to speak would be to elicit harsh judgements upon me because I knew my emotional state was not always the most controlled and I tended to get involved with very manipulative boys in my life who could too easily fake their personalities. Fear, anxiety, and silence. That was my life because of not knowing that I would not be judged.

This was the lesson I learned the hard way and one I endeavored to not have be the way my children would be raised. I learned through my own mistakes in the early years of my children's lives how I was becoming that which I had grown up around. I had to learn how to relinquish a need to control exactly how each and every conversation with my children evolved and instead just allow it to evolve as it was meant to evolve. Learning to listen, to just let children talk, and as they speak, hear the emotions residing beneath the surface and between the words spoken.

It seems such a simple undertaking, listening without judgement. It is what we all desire during conversations. Yet when we are in the adult versus child role in a conversation, we too often get caught up in the "_____knows better" scenario. Want to know a brutal truth? We don't always know better. It hurts to have to admit that, but it is important to bring to light.

Sometimes when we sit and discuss life, love, and happiness with our children, we don't always know better. We grew up in a completely different day and age, in a completely different way, than our children grew up. Admitting to them: *I am sorry, but on this matter, I truly don't know the right thing to say, the right advice to give,* sometimes is the best thing that you could say. Show them we are not infallible. Show them we care. Show them no matter what they come to us with, we will still love and support them, and **listen** intently to what they have to say.

My challenge for you:

1. **DROP YOUR EGO AT THE DOOR.**

The next time your son or daughter comes to you to tell you about whatever it is that Sally-says-a-lot has spouted off in the hallway between homeroom and second hour, drop your damn ego and just listen. Your ego is either going to sit and get in a tizzy about how meaningless the conversation at hand is, and you are likely to say something like, "This is so pointless. You know I have real world, real life problems. Bills and Grandma is sick, and the dog needs to be let out, and whatever the stuck up girl says, it doesn't really mean anything anyway because soon you are going to graduate, and she won't be in your life anymore." Don't allow your ego to have a place in that conversation. Remember that you too were that age, once upon a time, dealing with your own personal version of Sally, and wondering why your mom or dad couldn't simply listen to what it was that you were saying and thinking and feeling. Drop your ego and listen from your heart space.

2. **EMBRACE YOUR CHILD'S INSECURE NATURE.** Most of what your child is coming to you with during those moments revolve around a deep sense of insecurity. He or she is seeking approval for who they are because it is you they take their cues from. If you accept who they are, how they think, and what they feel, then they, in turn, learn how to accept themselves.

3. **LISTEN WITHOUT JUDGEMENT TO TALK WITH YOUR CHILDREN.** Combine the thoughts from the previous chapter with this chapter. Think about all your interactions to date with your children. Talk with them, talk to them,

and do so after you have sat down with them and listened to what it is they had to tell you about from their day. This will truly be one of the greatest gifts you can give them. In this way you will be showing them they matter. Their thoughts and emotions are being taken fully into consideration and you *care* about what they are telling you. That is what we all wish for when having conversations about the things in life that impact us. We want to know that what matters to us, what impacts us, matter to another human being. That we matter. Give this gift to your child so they will pay it forward with the next generation to come, and the cycle of silence will be broken.

7

What if you could go back to school, learn to dance, sing at the top of your lungs, take up macrame?

Okay, I have to admit right here and now that I do not know how to macrame. In fact, when I thought about this what if, I genuinely considered listing something like crocheting which is something I do know how to do. The question is not about the specifics listed, but the intention and thought behind it. What if you could do the thing that you keep telling yourself, "Someday I am going to_____."

Why are you waiting for some illusory "someday" to come to you? Are you expecting lightning to strike, to win the lottery, or for life to suddenly slow down so you can start something new? I am here to tell you that *someday* is today. Someday is not a far off future date, where life is suddenly flowing easily, and you have nothing left to worry about beyond what it is you envision yourself taking up. Someday is quite literally right now.

Back in 2018, I told David I wanted to learn to crochet. I even created the easiest *someday* situation to justify getting the materials I would need to learn how, Christmas. I told him that for Christmas that year, what I wanted more than anything was crochet materials. I wanted to learn this skill my Grandmother had been doing for years and utilizing as a means of gifting her loved ones. I wanted that to be me someday. Taking up the hook, as it were, for her when she passed and making blankets and doilies and all manner of different items to show the people I love, that I love them through the hard work I put into creating something with my own two hands. (That and I have an obsession with blankets, am always cold, and love combining colors.)

When I came to a point in which I decided I wanted to learn to read tarot and oracle cards, I found my way to affordable online courses, spending my days breaking my inner self down piece by piece through pulling cards over and over again. I learned through hard work, determination, and finding my way to the places, people, and things that would truly help me learn what I desired to learn. I didn't sit around waiting for something specific to come into my life to shine a light and indicate that RIGHT NOW was the exact right time for me to begin a new journey with a new passion.

What reasons are you giving for holding yourself back? Money, time, situations? The only thing holding you back right now, is you. If you have something in your heart, some burgeoning desire and passion growing within you that you want to develop and grow, take the leap into it. Jump into the unknown. Along my journey in life I have taken a detour from all I had known before, venturing into the unknown of Spirituality. Finding my route highlighted along the way by Spirit Guides and by God himself (or herself, however you see our great Creator). It was a route, a life, a passion I truly never saw coming into my life.

I had grown up in the Lutheran church. I went to Sunday School. I had my First Communion, Confirmation, was married, and baptized all of my children in the same church I had grown up spending every Sunday in. Suddenly I found myself learning about all the things my soul had been calling me to learn since I was a child. Challenging the pastor I had grown up listening to who had decided I was now damning my eternal soul because I love astrology, crystals, Reiki, tarot cards, and embraced my journey into Spirituality.

There was no set someday notion for me when it came to my Spirituality, there just was a right here, right now kickstart to my life going a new direction. There is no someday notion you are meant to be holding onto either. You are meant to know and recognize when there is something calling to you, it is calling to you for the simple fact it is what you are meant to do.

Following your heart can create fear, worry, and anxiety. I watched a YouTube tarot pick-a-card video once about living your life purpose from Roseology. I cannot remember the exact video it was, but the part sunk deep into my psyche from what she shared was, "When you are living your life purpose it is supposed to feel scary and exhilarating. You are going to be afraid of what you are doing and engaging in. This is how you are *supposed* to feel. It is the indicator

you are doing what you are meant to be doing."
(I am paraphrasing her to the best of my ability,
if you want to try to find the video, or receive
your own insights into your life through her
channeling, please go check her out on
YouTube.)

Feel that pulling to learning something.
Embrace it. Follow it. When you do, you are
opening doors to possibilities you couldn't
fathom prior. This is what it is meant to do for
you. How you are meant to live your life. Spirit,
God, the Creator, the Universe, whatever it is you
call your higher power, is waiting for you to take
that next step forward. You have dreams and
desires because they are meant to lead you
forward into a new life, a new you.

We are all living our lives, in the spiritual
community we like to say that we are spirits
having a human experience, but that in and of
itself is the buzzword needing directed focus:
EXPERIENCING. We are meant to experience

our lives. We are meant to delve deeply into the things that we want to see, hear, feel, learn, and do. It is all part of experiencing life. We all contain within us a spirit, an essence, a connection to the Divine Oneness that created us all in beautifully imperfect perfection. We are meant to feel. We are meant to learn. We are meant to grow.

Elbert Hubbard said, "Don't take life too seriously. You'll never get out alive." What poignant words. What truth. It seems almost ludicrous in its own way, while simultaneously being exactly the words we all need to hear, particularly when we are seeking to live a new experience. Don't be so serious about what it is that you want to do. Don't break yourself and your situation down, beating yourself up, telling yourself you are unworthy of this experience or that learning opportunity. If you want it, go after it with all you have.

My challenge for you:

1. **LEARN SOMETHING NEW.** Go out and learn something new. Why do you feel as though you need a classroom environment to learn and grow mentally and emotionally? What rule is there that your knowledge has to come from a certification or some overpaid piece of paper confirming you know what you know? Not one single person in the world has the right to tell you that your understanding and knowledge is lesser than that of another person's solely because they have a diploma and you do not if you have the ability and knowledge base demonstrated to them. We live in a society that puts far too much weight on classroom and by-the-book learning and doesn't take into consideration nearly enough the ability of a person to educate themselves. We expect school to educate everyone on all the things they are

expected to know, and by placing such high expectations upon the shoulders of everyone, we are crippling true knowledge and learning. So screw all of the societal standards put into place by stuffy old men and women who yearn for control over the minds of others due to their outdated ways of perceiving the world, flip the bird to the institutions touting themselves as the high and mighty ways of teaching life, and learn about life on your own terms. Experience education in the way that your heart is calling you to experience it.

2. **TAKE UP A NEW HOBBY.** What do you want to learn how to do? Perhaps you are the person who wants to learn macrame. Perhaps you, like me three years ago, feel the itch to learn how to crochet and create beautiful and warm blankets for yourself and for your family. Whatever it is that you want to do, go do

it. Learn to draw by drawing. Learn to crochet or read tarot cards or to build a giant castle out of playing cards for no other reason than that you want to. Do something for yourself that fuels a fire of creativity and passion in your life. When you do, you will see your life shifting all around you. You will feel happier, brighter, and more accomplished than you did before.

3. **STOP DEFEATING YOURSELF BEFORE YOU START.** We all do it from time to time. I wouldn't allow myself to try to write for years because what right did I have to write any sort of advice book? I don't have a college degree. There are no fancy letters at the end of my name. You know what I have? I have a higher than average, superior IQ, severe ADHD, and a life full of lessons just waiting to be put down on paper. That is

what I have. Why would that make me unqualified? It wouldn't, but I defeated myself before I started. Time and time again. It is a negative mindset that no longer serves who we are as a collective. It no longer serves who you are as a person. It doesn't serve your spirit. It doesn't serve your life. So, all the things it doesn't serve, combined with the fact that the only thing that would truly serve your life is to live it, inevitably means that what you are being called to do is to live. Don't tell yourself you can't. Don't give me, your mom, your spouse, nor yourself any reasons why you shouldn't and can't do this or that or the other thing. Just stop, and go live your life because I know you are meant to, you know you are meant to, and there is nothing else in the world you should be doing other than living your life.

8

What if you could still your mind and body in order to meditate?

I spent much of my twenties making excuses for why I was unable to meditate. "My anxiety won't allow me to. Who in their right mind can calm their brain down enough to meditate? Meditation doesn't work for me." All were arguments that I forced myself to believe. All were, forgive my crudeness, complete bullshit. I was filled to the brim with a pile of bullshit arguments to not try something because my inner world did not want me to "get better."

I lived a long time believing very negative things about my life, and not allowing for any kind of openness in thinking and being. It isn't something I am proud of, yet simultaneously, the act of healing and overcoming all of it are things I am deeply proud of myself for. I wouldn't have that pride in who I am and what I have learned if it were not for the state of being I was in prior. All things in life are experienced for the reason that we need to learn and grow from them. This is one area I truly did need to change and heal.

I suffered from Generalized Anxiety Disorder for much of my teenage years, going back even into my childhood. I worried about how I came off to other people, whether I was too loud, too emotional, too sensitive, too abrasive, too anything and everything. I always felt as though I was "too" and there were many people who would tell me just that.

In fourth grade I had a teacher who I idolized. I saw how he treated me and my classmates and felt as though he was the only adult who truly saw me. So when he decided to use me as a science experiment without telling me about it, I felt as though the "results" of his experiment were the end-all, be-all for who I am and what "too" I truly was.

We were taking a test, and he would drop his pencil on the floor, intentionally. Every time he dropped his pencil I would get up from my desk, pick it up, give it to him, sit back down, and continue taking my test. My grade on the test was a 100%, my score on his experiment landed me in the category of "too hyper" and he told my mom he believed I have ADHD. Now, let me qualify this a bit with the fact that he was correct, I do have ADHD, it is quite severe, and I don't respond well to medications, though I am on them. All things I am perfectly comfortable with admitting to the world because they are part of who I am. Yet, it was another "too" label and the first time I was old enough to be fully aware that my "too's" were becoming too much for other people to handle.

Now I was faced with the brutal truth, one in which I now outright will tell you to GET OVER IT, if you try to put it on my shoulders ever again, but back then, it was debilitating: *the only way to be loved and accepted by others was to never be myself.* I started compartmentalizing my personality. Overanalyzing each and every action and reaction I had.

Am I being too loud? Am I getting up too quickly? Am I being helpful or too hyper? I lived in a state of constant self-doubt, constant anxiety. Because of this interaction and the resulting mentality I lived with, I stopped being able to just be. My belief in being able to still my body and my mind was effectively destroyed before it was even able to begin in my life. I was nine and believed that I was "too hyper" and constantly doubted and analyzed every minute detail of my existence.

In 2020, I threw myself into crocheting. Making blankets and table runners, coasters and scarves. As I engaged in this activity I noticed that I could sit in one position without changing or moving for hours on end. I also noticed that I stopped thinking about who thought what of me, what appearance I was giving to the outside world, and whether or not I was "too" anything. What blissful freedom I found during those days. What release from the incessant hamster running on the wheel of my mind.

It was after this when I began noticing that through the act of sitting and crocheting my heart rate would slow, my blood pressure would normalize, and I wouldn't feel a need for my anxiety medications that I realized I had found a way to meditate. I would crochet and still my mind and my body. Then I began thinking about other activities that I would engage in that would have the same or similar results: doing sudoku puzzles and fill-in word puzzles also worked.

Hmmm, maybe there is something to this meditation stuff after all. Yes, yes there is. There is something to this meditation stuff. Meditation in its essence has been around since before written word. It has been a means of elevating one's consciousness, calming one's mind, and steadying one's heart. It also is a means of healing. Healing the mind-body-spirit connection. It brings us to center, brings us to balance, and helps us to align to a greater meaning and purpose in the world and within ourselves.

We can all too easily find excuses to not meditate. But, what if you could? What if what you do as a hobby is actually a form of meditation? What kind of nonsensical revelations can be found in thinking this way! David is an avid gamer. Something that truly used to, and still at times does, drive me up the walls bonkers. Mostly because in the beginning of our relationship I didn't understand why he was so addicted to something that I viewed as so frivolous. That was when we sat down and had a conversation about what purpose video games serves for him.

Video games are his escape. They are his way of winding down and shutting the incessant hamster in his mind down from running, running, running all the time. They are his crocheting. They for him serve as a means of meditation. He focuses on the task at hand in the game and in doing so does not think about the bills, the stressors in his work environment, and the discord that occurs with a house of four children with dominant personalities. Video games are how he decompresses after a long day of dealing with other people's concerns, and the rigors of his job.

We all have something we are able to access that allow us to open the door to stilling our minds and bodies. A means of meditating in our own way. There is no right or wrong way to do something that brings about a deeper sense of mental and emotional peace. We simply need to find what it is that work for us on a personal level.

My challenge for you:

1. **THINK ABOUT AND IDENTIFY YOUR "THING."** What do you do in your life that serves to slow your mind down? What are you able to do that keeps your body from flitting around from point A to point B to point C, D, E, etc.? Find what your "thing" is which helps you to be still for any duration of time. Find the moments in which you know you will not be consumed with thinking about what it is you need to do today, tonight, tomorrow. Find that thing in your own life. If you don't have one, find one.

2. **EMBRACE THE CHANGE.** Embrace the change of thinking and perceiving what it is you are engaging in to see it in

the light of "meditating." Allow yourself to be open to a new way of viewing an ancient activity in a modern age. Embrace the change of perspective on it.

3. **DEVELOP YOUR MEDITATION FURTHER.** Congratulations! You have identified what you do to slow your mind and body. You have found your open door to meditating. You've allowed yourself to embrace the thought process and perception of meditation being more than what it was originally. What a beautiful shift and change you have made for yourself. Now deepen your relationship with meditation. Try a new way of doing it because you know you are able to now. Growth happens when you seek to continue to better yourself. Growth happens when you continue to develop the skills you have into deeper, more meaningful ways of living your life. Don't

run from it, don't make excuses, just allow yourself to see what more you can do and be.

9

What if you could accept love to the depth you give it?

As an Empath, I love deeply, though I often feel as though I love others more than they love me. I often feel as though I am unable to be loved. I spent many years of my life believing I was not lovable nor capable of accepting love because it was always surface level and never the kind of love I would gift another with. I was faced with the reality of being loved as deeply as the love I was giving another when I began having struggles in my marriage with David.

He doesn't show love in the same way I do. It became a necessity for him and me to understand the love language we show and accept love through. There is a quiz online that will help you identify what your love language is. Truthfully, as of right now, I have never read *The Five Love Languages* by Gary Chapman. Despite not having read the book, I have a friend, Hope, who talked about the way that she shows love being through gifting others. It is how she shows that she loves me, she will show up randomly after not seeing me for months, and she will have the perfect gift. Always gifting me with things that show she knows who I am, what I love in the world, and a deep connection between us of intuitive knowing for what it is I need at that moment.

When David and I struggled with words versus actions, I said something in an offhanded thought during a long discussion about our marriage, "I half wish that I knew what your love language is so I could understand better." The next day when he was at work he texted me a screen shot of the results of his Love Language quiz. Deeply moved by this action, I went and did the same thing. Now I found the issues at hand that we were having so clearly and tangibly. My love language is actions, his is words.

We were having continual discord because he would say something and do something different. In my eyes, and because of a long traumatic lifetime filled with broken promises and actions that belied the words spoken to me, I equated the discord in David's words and actions with not loving me. I did not understand that his way of showing love was steeped in the beautiful, meaningful words he spoke to me.

Simultaneously, he did not understand, my questioning his love spawned directly from the fact that I see and give and accept love in the form of actions and quality time. I want someone to show me they love me through being present. Listening, conversing, and being undivided.

What I have always equated to neediness, is actually my Love Language.

Middle ground is the best way to work through the false perception of not being worthy of receiving love from another to the depth you give it. We are all different. We are all on different journeys in our lives and in these journeys we must find the common ground with the people we love in order to fully embrace the love we seek from another. Forgiveness is a big factor in all of this as well.

When you learn of something done by a person you love, if you are anything like me, you have a tendency to question why you are not worthy of the love you are giving to another. You question what your worth is, whether you are ever going to be loved how you love another person, and why, oh why, did the person you love hurt you. This wasn't done out of spite (usually, though I am sorry to say I have experienced in my first marriage many hurtful moments done out of deep hatred and spite, so I will allow for this to be a possibility in certain cases).

For the most part, if you love someone and they truly return your love with love of their own, they do not seek to hurt you emotionally with ill intent. It is done out of a lack of understanding, and perhaps, in a small way, short-sightedness. Forgiving the person for these facts will set your heart free. Forgiveness is the ultimate path to freedom.

My challenge for you:

1. **FORGIVE AND LET LIVE.** So you have been slighted. You have a sense of being betrayed. You feel as though the person you love just could not or did not love you in return. Forgive them. Perhaps you feel as though you were not forthcoming with your true emotions, did not give the love you deserve to receive. Whether this is because of a sense of lack

in your life (lack of worth, lack of love as a child, etc.) or because you were afraid that loving someone like that would only set you up for heartache, what you need to do right now in this moment is forgive. Forgive yourself and others. Let others live as they were made to live, and you too should live your life and your love as you were meant to live.

2. **GIVE YOUR LOVE FREELY WITHOUT EXPECTATION.** One thing fully in your hands is the kind of love that you give to others. I challenge you to not even think twice, just give your love freely. Do not attach an expectation of receiving that love back from another person, just love. Love is the most powerful force in the whole of the cosmos. It is where we are meant to live our lives from. It is the greatest gift we are capable of gifting to another person, animal, mineral (you get

my meaning here). Give your love. Give it to others, but be sure you give your love to yourself as much as, if not more than, you give to all the others in your life. Your loving heart is where your true beauty shines, radiant upon this world, and the world needs more of the love you have in it.

3. **FIND YOUR LOVE LANGUAGE, OPEN COMMUNICATION, AND UTILIZE THESE TRUTHS DAILY.**
What is your manner of giving love to another? How do you show yourself love? Find your love language. Whether you choose to do this through an online quiz, through reading *The Five Love Languages*, or through personal evaluation of your manner of giving and receiving love, find it, identify it, then be completely open about it. Communication, full-frontal honesty,

complete transparency and love are yours to give, yours to receive. Finding how you operate on a heart based level will open the door for deepening of love between you and other people, and your heart will blossom beautifully, as will all things in your life as a direct result. We have all heard of the Butterfly Effect in one way or another. (Some of us simply think it is a movie starring Ashton Kutcher.) To reduce it to the simplest manner of understanding, it is about the ripple effect of a seemingly small action that spans the whole of the globe. A butterfly flaps its wings on one side of the world and the shift in the air causes a hurricane in the other side of the world. Though it may seem extreme, when you find your love language, open communication, and utilize both these truths every day of your life you create a powerful ripple effect through everything in your life. You are setting the standard of worth, love, and transparency that calls for others to respond in kind to you.

10

What if you could walk away from toxicity and never look back?

My life was consumed for years with toxicity. I was in a loveless, abusive marriage to a man who I loved with all my heart, and he hated me in equal measure. I stopped believing in any sense of freedom from his toxicity. The night he told me he was done with our marriage; I believed my life was over. Clearly, I was woefully mistaken at the time. What I didn't realize back then was I was being granted a ticket out of toxicity and into freedom to live my life on my terms, for myself.

Sweet, sweet freedom. Yet, I did not leave the toxicity behind. We have two children together, tied to each other in a new way, a way that kept the lines of manipulation and cruelty open; at least, that is what I believed at the time. The truth is I did not see the freedom for another five years. This is because I needed to heal from the pain, the manipulation, the control. I needed to take the time to truly allow myself to see that I was and am free from him.

About two years after my divorce to "George" I wrote a post on Facebook. I talked about all the changes I had undergone since the day I kicked him out of the house after learning of his affair with a woman I believed to be my friend. I set the post to be public. He and I were no longer friends on Facebook which meant the only way for him to see the post would be for it to be public. I was, as my fourth grade teacher once did to me, doing a sort of science experiment. I sensed he was, for lack of better terminology, stalking me online.

Twenty minutes. The post was up for twenty minutes before he set in on me. "If you're feeling inspirational, keep it off Facebook. I don't need to hear from my friends about you talking about us on Facebook." I could feel the anger and hatred radiating off the message I received, the level of toxicity and control he was trying his damnedest to seep back into my life. What a radiant light I shone in response, at least in my opinion. My response to him was beautiful, "The best part of not being married to you anymore is that you don't have control over what I do and don't do. You don't get to shut me up anymore."

I am so proud of that version of myself. She was naïve about how much control George still had, but damn it, she was standing up for herself, standing up for me. She didn't see, couldn't have seen, that she was still allowing George to control her, to have a say, to have the ultimate say, in how she saw herself. He still held the power over her because she was still allowing him to have that power.

It would take me until 2021 (14 years since we met, 13 years since the abuse began) before I quite literally told George he was abusive, manipulative, and projecting all his negative personality traits outward on another person, *me*. He still, to this day, believes he is utterly untouchable. He believes he holds more power over the judicial system, the Child Protection System, and over me. He believes all of these things because of a grand injustice from the courts when my daughter wasn't allowed a voice in the courtroom during our custody battle.

The true reasoning behind her not being allowed a voice and a say over her life, George objected and stated he was willing to fight over the course of months to have her testimony stricken, and would fight tooth and nail for her to not sit on the stand.

The hardest part of court in December 2020, was the judge calling my daughter to the stand, swearing her in, creating an illusion that she was going to be allowed to have her voice and testify, her father's crocodile tears, and the judge swearing her in solely to tell her he was not going to allow her to have a voice. Score one for George's toxicity and manipulation. Score one for his fallacy of invincibility. Score zero for justice, honor, integrity of the judge in the courtroom that day. Score zero for my daughter and her faith in the powers that be. Score zero for freedom and release from abuse.

So how can I sit here and ask the question what if you could walk away from toxicity and never look back? How can I ask this if I am still inured in it on a regular basis? Trust me when I tell you, I am not being hypocritical here. I no longer allow George to pass the blame onto another person. I understand there were factors and people I held no control over in that courtroom. I understand those things, and I also know that George has no power over me anymore.

There is a scene in the movie, The Lord of the Rings: The Two Towers, in which the king of Rohan is on his throne, possessed in a way by Sauron. He looks at Gandalf and says, "You have no power here, Gandalf Stormcrow." (Okay, I am a Tolkien and LOTR nerd, I own the title proudly.)

Whenever George attempts to tell me what my life is meant to look like, what I am and am not "allowed" to do, think, and/or say, I can't help but think of that moment in the movie. I want more than anything during those moments to be a complete smartass and tell him, "You have no power here, George Jackhole."

Jackhole is one of my favorite combo names. It is a way of combining Jackass and asshole. It is not kind, but we cannot always be kind in life. Sometimes we need to create a name that brings about giggles to make the pain of endurance something to laugh at. Sometimes we just need to be able to call someone a name without fear of repercussions from them because they have done the same to us more times than we can count.

I am a person who continually worries about what kind of Cause and Effect, what kind of Karma, I am creating with my actions. So I try my hardest to not call another person a name, to not be mean, to not be judgmental, while simultaneously being transparent and brutally honest. The brutal honesty here, calling George a Jackhole is far nicer than I could be to him considering.

I will never judge if you feel the need to name someone a name which helps you to feel more in your power. The only caution I will give is to be sure you are not standing in the power of cruelty and ego-centered manipulation. That makes you and me no better than the toxic abusers we are trying to break free from.

I could go on and on talking about all the ways George manipulated and created toxicity in my life, but then would I not be hypocritical in nature? This is about how to get away from it, rise above it, walk away from it, lock it up, throw away the key, and burn the whole house of toxicity to the ground so there is nothing left to even attempt to look back on. This is about you standing firm in your worth and your power and screaming at the top of your lungs to the heavens above, "ENOUGH IS ENOUGH! I AM WORTH MORE THAN THIS! I DESERVE BETTER, AND DAMN IT, I DEMAND MY WORTH!"

Lighter fluid applied, match lit, toss it on the remnants of the sad, scared, manipulated version of yourself from the past and burn it to ashes. Rise up like the phoenix regaining its life and wings out of the licking, fiery flames. You are the phoenix. You no longer need to live that life.

You have learnt the lessons you were meant to learn through the situations, and now you are being called to grown, change, burn it down, step into the flames, and cleanse out the negativity and toxicity from your mind, heart, and soul.

If you have a George, you can break free of that cycle. You can free yourself, free your past self, your inner child, your actual child, your actual soul. Freedom is yours because you now know you are worth more. It matters not what anyone else says, what does your heart say? What your heart says, not your head, not your anxiety, not your fear, for all those things lie to you and your heart tells you nothing but truth and love, those are the words you need to hear and heed right now.

My challenge for you:

1. **IDENTIFY WHERE YOUR LIFE IS IMPACTED BY TOXICITY.** This is one section in which the steps, the challenges,

I give to you are not a pick and choose, do out of order kind of thing. This is more important. First, you need to take a step back, whether physically and mentally, or just mentally. Step back from the people and the things in your life. What people, what activities, what places are you engaging with and in on a regular basis? How do those interactions and engagements make you feel? Are you drained, tired, insecure, etc. from them? If any of those feelings are applicable to your situation, then you have found toxicity. Now you are able to see more clearly where the toxicity is sourced from, and what impact it is having upon you on a regular basis.

2. **FIND YOUR TRUTH.** What is your truth? Are you feeling things about yourself and your life accurately before, during, and after engaging with your

sources of toxicity? When you search for your truth, you have to remember that no one else, not me, not your mom, not your pastor, not your spouse, are qualified to tell you *your truth*. Only you know what you are worth. Only you know whether the things you feel amongst the sources of your toxicity are an accurate representation of who you are. Find your truth of self, your truth from your heart. Live and love yourself solely from the space of your heart, and in doing so, you will find your truth.

3. **BURN IT DOWN, CLEANSE IT, AND NEVER LOOK BACK.** You found your toxic patterning, you found your truth, your voice, your way forward. Now burn the bridge between you now and the version of your life that was back then. It is your time to shine, your time to live for you. Let it all go, cleanse it in a

metaphorical blaze (for real, I am not encouraging you to go burn down an actual house here). Everyone deserves a phoenix risen moment in their life. Everyone deserves freedom from the toxicity plaguing their life. So break yourself free, and cleanse your being in flames. There are some amazing YouTube cleansing meditations to help with this. I personally love to do Violet Flame meditations. They always leave me feeling energized and ready to face anything and everything that may come my way again. Do not continue to look back at the old version of who you were, doing the things you used to. Become a new version of yourself. Shining and radiant, free of the shadowy toxicity from your past.

11

What if you could stand in your own power and declare yourself to the world?

I have talked about standing in your power, you hear it all the time in the spiritual community. You hear it in the self-help section of your local bookstore. You hear it wherever self-motivation is found. Finding your own power and declaring yourself to the world, well, that is another story entirely.

Before I began writing my blog, Monica Anderson, the Kismet Chemist, before I began writing *Chemistry with Kismet: Journeying into the Self to Heal the Mind*, before all of the life changes I have undergone, if you had asked me who I am, I would have told you what hats I wore and who I was to other people. I was a mother, a wife, an ex-wife, chronically ill, tired constantly, in immense pain daily. I was a reader, and at times I would even claim to be a writer, even though back then I had a lot of empty notebooks, barely formed ideas, and only the faintest whisps of a dream.

Personal power was a foreign concept to me. I was leaving my power solely to those around me. They were the ones I allowed to dictate my full worth. Whether I was loved hinged upon someone else. Thankfully, the same Christmas I was gifted with crochet materials, I was also gifted with a beautiful Celtic Cross leatherbound journal, and a book written by Jeff Goins called *You're a Writer, So Start Acting Like One*. David knew my lifelong dream was to be a published author, and every step of our relationship he has spent his time and energy encouraging me to write.

Never once along this process has he told me, "Why are you doing this? It isn't like you can make anything of yourself." It is not who he is. He would tell me, after me sending a long meaningful book-length text message to him about one thing or another, "You really should write a book."

As much love and encouragement as I was given by David, it would never be enough. Through no fault of his own, his words did not hold the weight he wished for. This is because I needed to find within myself the strength and resolve to stand in my power and declare myself to the world as an author. He could not do that for me. I had to get over my damn self and stop making excuses.

I write so I am a writer. I hit the publish button every single time one of my blog posts go live, therefore I am a published author. I own the domain to my website, and have created my own business name, so I am a business owner. None of these things I have done, nor person I have become are the result of the things said to me by another person, they are pieces of the whole of who I am, part of my own personal power.

All these things I set out to do and become were sourced directly from my soul. Parts of who I have always known I was meant to be. You have parts of yourself lying dormant within you, barely sleeping beneath the surface, waiting for you to bring them into the light of day, dust them off, and become YOU. Standing fully in all the things you could potentially accomplish, because you have the power to become YOU.

What are you waiting for? What is the "thing" you know you are put on this world to do, be, embody? Go! Go now! Do not wait one more second of one more day. Stand in who you are, firmly in your power. Go outside with your bare feet in the grass, ground yourself, pull strength from the ground below your feet, all the way up to the crown of your head, your crown chakra. Stand out in the sun, firmly planted on this Earth and plant the seeds in the physical realm of your spiritual self.

While you stand there, I want you to shout at the top of your lungs, without a care for Nosy-Nancy-Next-Door and what she may or may not tell the women at the church bazaar next Wednesday, "HERE I AM WORLD! I AM (SHOUT YOUR NAME HERE) AND I AM HERE TO STAY! I AM A (INSERT WHO YOU ARE, WHAT YOU ARE GOING TO BECOME IN YOUR LIFE HERE) AND NO ONE CAN STOP ME! I AM ME!"

You have now completed a personal ritual to stand in your power and declared yourself to the world, quite literally. What you plant in your own mind and in the energy of the Universe, it has power. You have power. We all have power.

We are meant to own that power within ourselves and allow it out to play, allow it to transform our Selves and our lives.

Declarations have been used for generations, millennia. When it came to the New World, the freedom of our country, it was the Declaration of Independence. It is what every red-blooded teenage boy is meant to do on some grand stage in front of his friends, opening himself to all manners of mockery, when he falls in love. Declare himself in love with a girl. It is the teenage way of asking another to prom these days. It is how an expectant mother tells the world that she is going to make her dream of birthing and raising tiny humans into functional people. We declare things every day of our lives. Some declarations are more grandiose than others, but they are used day in and day out, regardless.

If you are going to stand in your power, you should declare yourself to the world. It should be your grandest declaration you make in your life. Why? Because you are worthy of the grandest everything! You are a masterpiece, your dreams meant to be made manifest, and your soul a beautiful piece of artistry meant to be shared openly with others, declared as your own, your truth.

My challenge for you:

1. **GET GROUNDED AND SHOUT TO THE HEAVENS.** Do you want me to walk you through this again? I will. Did you think I was posturing when I wrote it earlier? I promise you; I was not. Go outside in your skivvies if you must. Who cares beyond you? Just go do it! Stand firm in the grass, let the sun rest its beautiful, gentle rays upon your shoulders, feeling the support from the Earth and guidance from the heavens, and shout your declaration of personal power and Self to the world. Now is your time!

2. **LIVE IN YOUR POWER.** Live your life on your own terms. Same as the first chapter, make no excuses, no qualifications. Say, "Yes," when you want to say yes. Say, "No," when you want to say no. Do not explain or qualify yourself. Live your life fully in who you are and what you know you are capable of being. Live in your power. You deserve it. You have earned it. You were made for it.

3. **LIVE IN FULL AUTHENTICITY AND DECLARATORY NATURE, DAILY.** Live in the fullness of your authentic self, your authentic truth every single day. Make your every action a declaration to the world, "This is who I am, and this is what I do. I make no apologies for it, and you should live as I do." Make your life a declaration, showing the Universe how truly committed you are to YOU. Prove to the nay-sayers, to the little liar in your

head known as anxiety, and to the ones who sought to take your power for their own, that you know your worth, your purpose, and your meaning and you are ready to stand firm in it every day of your life. Show the world just what your worth is, measured solely with your own yardstick and no one else's. Who has the power? You do. Be your own cheerleader, your own Queen, your own King. Be your full authentic self and declare over and over and over again who you are. Why are you doing this? Because you want the world to see just how powerful you are, just how worthy and lovable and loving and talented and capable you really are. Be you, overcome. Overcome through the simple art of standing in your power and being who you were meant to be all along. Be who you know yourself to contain within.

12

What if you could go back to high school and live those days all over again?

My high school years were marred by an abusive boyfriend, the boy next door being head over heels in love with me, a stepfather who simply didn't want kids around him (namely me), and being a teenage mother. They were filled to the top with rumors about what a slut and whore I was, perpetuated by adults and teenagers alike. I was the focus for many reasons, because of being a teenage mother, because my best friends were guys, because I was the "new girl."

I never fought back, so I was an easy target. I have had, over the last couple months, many conversations about whatifs. This topic came up recently with one of my former classmates who moved before our senior year of high school. I always viewed her as uniquely herself. She was smart without being overbearing, wore clothes that were just her, and seemed untouchable in persona to me. In fact I saw her in a group of three girls in our class all of the same caliber. Girls who didn't care what the fashion trends were, didn't care if anyone made fun of them for being smart, they lived life on their own terms. How was I to know they were crippled with as much insecurity and self-doubt as I was?

I am convinced that the people who truly wish to go back and relive high school fall into two categories:

1. Those who succeeded in high school and faltered later in life.

And

2. Those who were riddled with insecurities in high school, and made something of themselves after.

I fall directly in the second class of people. High school to me could have been so much more than it was, if only I had had the advice from the previous chapter. Instead I had labeled my worth and potential for popularity on what I wore, whether I was active in sports, what I read, who I was friends with. It was like living life in a constant beauty contest, and I did not have enough Vaseline for my teeth, nor did I know nearly enough ways to straighten, tease, and curl my hair. I was not a makeup person, and did not feel as though I was skinny or pretty enough to be a popular girl, and I definitely lacked the right last name for the small town I lived in.

Growing up, living my life outside of that world, I now see, none of those things mattered.

My name, my hair, my makeup, all are simply window dressing and unreasonable ways of valuing a person. High school is a dog-eat-dog world, and the way it was back then has not improved to how it is now. Girls fight over boys. Boys are as clueless as they have ever been. The faculty is tired, worn, and ready for whatever school break is coming up next.

What we need to consider instead of going back and reliving those days is how we are better equipped to use the experiences we had to change the way our children go through their high school experience. Are you going to tell your children your glory days tales and expect them to live up to those same standards? Are you going to baby step them forward in everything and go to war with the school board if you deem some treatment unjust? Are you going to teach them superiority or equality?

No matter what you experienced, living your life from the state of whatif I went back, whatif I did it differently, whatif, whatif, whatif. Don't live your life wondering whatif I did this or that, whatifs are so destructive. Live from a place of having truly learned from what you did or did not do during your time and encourage your children and the next generation to live in a different way. Encourage your child to be more accepting and inclusive.

Stop buying makeup for your thirteen year old daughter, and encourage her to befriend the loner girl in the corner, who everyone sneers at because she enjoys reading and wearing clothes from consignment stores. Encourage your son to ask out the girl who will never be asked to prom instead of the popular girl, because everyone deserves to spend a night feeling like a princess and being treated as such.

Encourage your child to set their sights on learning, experiencing, and living life with kindness and love as early as possible. These are the lessons we should have learned from the cruelty and bullying we have seen both during our own time and during the trials and tribulations of our children in high school. Don't think about going back and redoing this action or that behavior, and instead talk about those feelings with the next generation.

It is also important to remember we are not meant to live vicariously through our children. We are meant to live in awe of who they grow to be, taking the credit when it is due for the things we have taught them along the way, the growth we helped to facilitate. We are not meant to make them be cheerleaders, on the pom squad, competitive swimmers or dancers, basketball players, Prom King and Queens, because that is who we were or who we wish we were. We are meant to nurture every facet of their individuality, in every stage of their life, and teach them to live from a place of higher thought processes, and oneness of all.

Truthfully, I spent a long time wondering whatif, when reflecting back upon my high school years. Whatif I had stayed in basketball and cheerleading. Whatif I had called my boyfriend on his threat to ruin my reputation in town if I were to break up with him before starting school, and did it anyway. My reputation was ruined as it was, no one really knew me back then, especially not myself. Whatif I had done it differently.

There is no sense in wondering whatif because everything that we experience in our lives is what we were meant to experience. They are moments brought into our world so we will learn, grow, and change for the better. I would not change my high school years. Without them how they played out, I would not have my beautiful daughter. My son would not have the life nor the parents he does. There would be so many beautiful people and moments in life that would be nonexistent in my life without having lived high school exactly as I did.

My challenge for you:

1. **STOP LOOKING BACK.** Stop reflecting back and wondering whatif when it comes to your high school years. You lived the way you were meant to, as the person you were meant to be. The reasoning for it, only you will find out. Your lessons are your own, they are what you were meant to learn, how you were meant to grow. No one can take those moments away from you. The only thing that could potentially remove them would be to go back and live it all over again, doing it differently the second time around. You wouldn't be who you are today, you wouldn't be who you are meant to be right here, right now. You would become a doppelgänger of who you are now, and your life would be

completely different with no guarantee of it being better than it is now.

2. **LIVE IN THE NOW.** As a society we are spending entirely too much time focusing on the past or the future and not nearly enough focusing on the present moment. The here and now is the only time we are guaranteed in the world. Stop looking one way or another and see all that you have in front of you, because that is all that matters. The now.

3. **LEAVE HIGH SCHOOL TO THE HIGH SCHOOLERS.** Stop reminiscing about the "glory days," of football, basketball, and homecoming. Sure you were a stud, a queen, the coolest of the cool, but it is time to realize that *was* your life, but it is not anymore. Those days you get to live one time, and one time only. Now you get to live your life for yourself, and not for the social status given to you

by the powers that be. Learn from how you lived your life and grow from it, allowing yourself to change and flux and change from who you were into who you are, leaving high school to the high schoolers living it now.

13

What if you could eat that piece of cake without feeling guilty?

"Let them eat cake!" Man, oh man, do I love the French for that phrasing. We live in a society in which we are being scrutinized for everything we put in our body. Is the flour all natural, did you use cage-free eggs? Did you use eggs? Why would you put something with such a high carb content in your body? A moment on the lips, forever on the hips.

Gah! The audacity! Let them eat the damn cake! Every fad diet is rich in what to do and what not to do. When your body needs something it will tell you through your cravings.

When you want to eat that piece of cake, just eat it. You know what your body truly wants and needs. When you punish yourself over and over again because it isn't helping your body look as it is meant to look in your mind's eye or by societal standards, you are in effect starving yourself.

I am a spiritual person. I live my life and my faith on the terms that I deem worthy for me. I also used to weigh 220 pounds at 5 foot 7 inches tall, with a body mass index of 34.5, aka "seriously fat." I was unhappy and drowning my sorrows in sweets, carbs, and sweet wine. I was starving my soul and drowning my body in unhealthy foods, and every single bite I felt guilty and beat myself up for.

Through my spiritual awakening, I quit drinking completely. Then went soda of all sorts. Then cakes and cookies, candy and all things sugary. This wasn't because of a fad diet and following whatever spirituality told me I was meant to eat, instead it was about me following the prompting of my body. I was talking to Amanda Dunn, a YouTube content creator known for The Dunn Creative, and an author, just last night about what foods she eats. She told me about her food based spiritual journey and we compared it to each other.

Though my style of eating is different from hers, I felt no judgement from her on what I choose to put in my body. In fact, she put a title to it which was inherently exactly what it was I needed to hear: Intuitive eating. We are all spiritual beings having a human experience. I believe this with everything within me. This is because I have experienced unexplainable to the human mind, situations. I have had visions, astral projected, made predictions and witnessed them coming to pass in exacting detail. (I was having a conversation with my sister just this morning about my prediction of her becoming my sister, made months prior, and the fact that it has just recently come true.)

I share these things not to brag, but to help you understand why the human experience is so important. Experiencing life in this world is about each and every interaction we have, including the interactions we have with food. We are meant to tease our taste buds, to flow with the flavors found in abundance in the world. So let them eat cake, let yourself eat cake.

If your body and your tastebuds are telling you to eat or drink something particular, then try it, taste it, experience it. This is part of our purpose here. People pay exorbitant amounts of money to go to a five star restaurant to eat two bites per plate of food, simply because the flavor combination sets not only their mouths but also their souls ablaze.

Italians know that food is equatable to sex, to a religious experience. There is a crude phrasing called a foodgasm. We call it such because it sends tingles and shockwaves of pleasure from our mouths to our stomachs and triggers our brains to feel joy, happiness, and pleasure. Just as we would having an orgasm, this one is done through food. Every facet of being a human involved experiences in some way, shape and form. Eating the decadent, chocolate-filled, chocolate slathered piece of cake, well, that is a part of it.

My challenge for you:

1. **CALL A CHEAT DAY.** We are all perpetually on some sort of diet it would seem. Call a cheat day. Eat what you cannot get off your mind. Why am I encouraging this? Because with it on your mind constantly there leaves little room for anything else to come into your thoughts. If you are continually watching cookies dancing through your head, you are not focusing on the road in front of you when you are driving, you are not seeing the joyful faces of your children when you greet them after your day, and

you are not able to listen to your intuition. You are consumed with a sense of lack because you are denying yourself.

2. **TEACH YOURSELF SELF-CONTROL VERSUS COMPLETE WITHOLDING.** When you are changing anything in life, going cold turkey is more of a hindrance than helpful. Again, I feel the need to reiterate, if you are an addict and you are quitting drinking or doing drugs, this is not the case. I am not a medical professional, please do not run to your addiction counselor saying, "Monica Anderson said in her book I can take another shot," because no, no, no! When you are dieting, changing your life for the better, going off of anything like cookies, cakes, candy, soda, even television shows, you need to recognize what can happen when you completely withhold everything you have been accustomed to. Self-control

is about recognizing when to say no and when to say yes. It is about following the intuition that is a gift we all contain.

3. **THROW GUILT OUT OF THE WINDOW**. Obviously, I am talking in metaphors here, but I just had an image of a little boy with a rock painted with the word "Guilt" being thrown through a kitchen window. When I tell you to throw guilt out of the window, I mean for you to cease shaming yourself for your desires. Learning self-control entails relieving yourself from guilt and shame as well. We are not meant to live with guilt and shame. It is what locks up our throat chakras, so we are unable to properly speak about that which we desire for our lives. We cannot speak truth, we cannot live in authenticity, if we are encumbered by guilt and shame. They do not serve

your highest good, and you deserve a life lived for your highest good.

14

What if you could say, "I love you," hear it spoken in response, and trust in it being a mutual emotion?

Trust is a difficult emotion, it is a difficult concept, for a person who has been the victim of trauma, manipulation, narcissism, and abuse. When it comes to love, unless you love yourself, know you are capable of giving and receiving love, and trust the person you love to love you back, you will struggle with the honesty in the words spoken.

I spent many years with a man who truly was not capable of loving another human being.

He says he loves his children, he said he loved me, but to be loved by him was to feel his anger and disapproval, to disappoint and be abused. It was all I knew of "love," for many years, and when I was freed from the constraints of his "love" I discovered what love really looks like. I also discovered the necessity of loving oneself first before being able to receive true love from another.

When David first told me he loved me, it was not the way it should have been. We were midway through an argument because we were in a fraught situation and trying to decide if we should be together. It was a month after my divorce was finalized, there was another man showing interest in me, I was broken down from everything in my life being uprooted, and here came the man I already loved and was trying my best not to, telling me he loved me. I didn't trust it at all. I didn't trust him. I didn't trust love.

I didn't know how to trust any of it because the man before him who told me I was loved had hit me, used sex as a weapon, gaslighted me, drugged me, and all manner of depraved things. There was not a shred of trust remaining in my heart or soul. Yet, I loved the man who just told me he loved me. What's a woman to do?

We struggled through the next six months trying to decide to even begin a relationship. Telling each other that we loved each other, together while not truly being together. It was hard, and painful. Once more another man came into my life, and I felt as though if I threw my all into the potential for a relationship with someone else I would be able to leave David behind and move forward in my life. The heart doesn't work that way. The other man who had come into my life told me he loved me as well, but it was done after there was manipulation. I was staring down the barrel of being with someone who was just like George, my ex-husband, all because I didn't know how to trust the love David was telling me he felt for me.

Everything came to a wicked head when I decided to run a train through my personal life. Everything I had built after my divorce; I was tearing down. I was hurting people left and right with little care as to who was harmed in the process. Lying, crying, and then lying more so the people who loved me would grow to hate me as much as I hated myself. It wasn't healthy. I don't suggest it.

David came over midafternoon to pick up a pair of shorts and a DVD that was still at my house. Maybe they were items he truly needed, but I believe it was more the fact that he needed some sense of closure with me. I was sick to my stomach waiting for him to get to my house, waiting to see him, waiting to feel as dead inside when I looked at him as I felt when he wasn't there. Again, my heart was leading the way, and my mind was blown away with the reality I had no choice but to face.

David walked in my front door, one look between us and we were both in tears. David doesn't cry. Not unless there is a dog on YouTube or Facebook's video feed screaming in fear at its own farts or jumping and failing gloriously in an attempt to catch a ball or a frisbee. He jokes now about how when he needs a good cry, he will put on a comedic dog video and laugh until tears roll down his face. For my actions to have elicited tears in his eyes, it was a knife to the heart. I had thrust a knife in his back, into my own heart, with my own narrow-minded, selfish actions.

All this was done because I simply could not trust love. David was an innocent bystander to my destruction. His tears led to a torrent of confessions from me I was not prepared to share. It was how he always had impacted me. From the night I met him, four days after kicking George out of my house, the very night I asked George for a divorce, I had for no explainable reason, felt a sense of safety with who I am and what I was thinking and feeling when I was alone and talking to David.

This all occurred during a time I was refusing outright to acknowledge and embrace my own intuition. I was not willing to consider the whys of any of it. I did not want to pop any bubble of having a person I could trust. Yet trusting him with my deep-seated darkness and trusting him with my heart, those were two very different things. I had to learn, through many discussions, many arguments, and a lot of his patience, that I could trust in the love he was presenting to me.

Empaths are a special variety of people. Most I have met and spoken with, struggle deeply with trusting in other people. This is because we inherently love all people and all things, and we are willing to continually give second, third, fourth, hundredth chances when we love a person. We will allow for our psyches and trust to be broken time and again because we see the underlying goodness contained within broken shells of ego-centered humanity. We are lights in the darkness, and we struggle deeply.

Everyone is meant to love and receive love in return. Love is meant to be part of the human experience. It takes a lot to acknowledge this fact, because it effectively calls into question the distrust we tend to feel after being hurt. Living from the heart is what is always called for. I talk about living from the heart center, or heart space, a lot. I cannot tell you exactly how to do that, for I do not have the proper words for it.

Everyone lives from their heart in different ways. They find themselves struggling with how to feel about another person, likely because they are struggling with how they feel about themselves. Living from the heart is a deeply personal action. One in which only you will know if you are in your heart center, living from your heart space. You have to trust yourself, and what you *feel* over what you are thinking.

My challenge for you:

1. **IDENTIFY THE FEELINGS COMING FROM YOUR HEART.** When you are trying to make a decision about trust and love, you need to sit with yourself, and only yourself. Do not consult another person, they do not know how you truly feel, and their advice will be clouded by both their own personal experiences as well as the love they have for you and sense of needing to protect you. You need to sit in a quiet space and allow yourself to feel. Feel deeply into yourself. Feel deeply into your emotions. Leave the thoughts behind, and just go based on feeling. This is how you identify the feelings coming from your heart.

2. **FIND TRUST.** Finding trust is the hardest part of all of this. You have to know your worth. I am here to tell you that you are worthy of the love you have always dreamt of receiving from another person. You are worthy of the depth of love you give. You can tell another person, "I love you," hear back from them, "I love you too," and trust their love is their truth. I cannot lie and tell you it is easy to do this, but it is freeing. You deserve to be free to love and be loved. You deserve to be free to trust again. You deserve all the love in the world. You now need to trust.

3. **DON'T HOARD YOUR LOVE AWAY FROM THE WORLD.** Holding your love within you, being fearful of releasing it into the world, creates a blockage within your heart chakra. Your energy centers become unbalanced and are knocked out of harmony. Internally you are out of sync

with your true nature, Love. This again speaks to the saying, "Be the change you want to see in the world," spoken by the incredibly insightful Mahatma Ghandi. Be the love you want to see in the world by giving the love you want to receive.

15

What if you could change your life to exactly how you envision it?

Close your eyes, take a few deep breaths, now think about what you want your life to look like. What are you picturing? What do you need to do to create this life? This is the first step into living that life. Envisioning what you wish for, seeing it in your mind's eye, you are giving yourself the permission to dream, to be, to become. It is a powerful tool in the manifestation arsenal, visualization.

On the afternoon of June 30, 2020, I was talking to David about setting goals for my 33rd year of life. When it came to visualizing what I wanted my life to look like a year from then, the first thing I saw was myself, a published author. It felt unreachable, untouchable, yet it was on my list of goals. I wanted to write a book. I wanted it, desired it, with every fiber of my being. I of course wanted a multitude of material items to change, but this to me was not a material change, it was a spiritual change. This was a desire I had from my youngest years, and I had in that moment decided I was setting the goal for me to accomplish it once and for all. If I was never meant to be an author, then the attempt at writing a book would serve to sway me in another direction in life.

I made the goal list, and then I did nothing, for months. It was not until November 6, 2020, and suddenly words were flowing out of my mind, and I could no longer justify not putting them down on paper. I sat at my computer and spent hours, days, months typing. Editing, formatting, setting everything, and then going back at it again. I burnt out, walked away, then continued to come back to it. It was like a drug, an addiction, something I *needed* to complete. By the end of January 2021 the book had a beginning, middle, end, and I had done so many passes on it, I couldn't read it as it was anymore.

This is when I hit my first major blockage. I spiraled in deep-seated fear. *Am I watching my lifelong goal ending right now? Am I really meant to only come this far and now I need to walk away?*

I studied and became a Reiki Master. Studied Animal Reiki and was attuned to it. Started considering going down the path of healer, yet everything within me kept coming back to writing. I yelled and screamed and cried in broken sobs time after time. Yelling at God, yelling at the Universe, yelling at my Spirit Guides. "THIS IS ALL I HAVE EVER WANTED!

WHY ARE YOU TAKING THIS AWAY FROM
ME?!"

I couldn't see the truth: I was the only
person standing in my own way. When you
desire something with your heart, you are the
one that has to put in the work, and then you
throw it out to the Universe with the strict
intention of watching it be made manifest,
trusting it will happen as it is meant to.

The Universe wants you to show it exactly
what you want in life. It wants to work with you
to manifest your dreams into a reality. This is
what we are meant for in life. Working hand in
hand with the Universe to create the lives of our
dreams. We are meant to dream bigger, be
greater, and change our lives and those of others
through being our true selves. I am now
approaching my 34th birthday, and this is my
second book. Two books written in one year. Two
books published in one year.

All the words and thoughts and stories floating around in my mind for years, all the things I had until this year been refusing to put down on paper, have now come flooding out of me without a stopper to stem the tide. Everything I have been meaning to share with the world, it is now my time. Why? Because I set that intention, and I put in the work.

One of the hardest parts of "putting in the work," is doing shadow work. There is not one single soul walking this Earth that can make you do the shadow work you need to do to create the reality you envision. You have to take the reins, becoming an active participant in your life, and work through all the parts of yourself you have been repressing and hiding away.

Everyone does shadow work in their own way. There is no right or wrong way of pulling up the negative thoughts contained in your mind, blocking your soul from shining outward through your life. For me, it began with journaling, reading, and tarot cards. Utilizing them to break down the parts of my mind I loathed dusting off and evaluating, I knew the only way forward was to go back and heal what needed healing. For you it could be through talk therapy. It could be through hypnosis and regression therapy. Perhaps you are the person who heals the best through stillness and meditation.

Whatever you medium for shadow work and healing, I implore you to do what you feel called to do. Work on yourself so you can work on building the life you desire, the dreams you wish for, and the goals you are capable of accomplishing.

My challenge for you:

1. **SHADOW WORK.** Is there any surprise this is my first challenge? If so, you don't know me well enough quite yet. Don't worry, that will change. How that will

change is when you start doing the work on your subconscious mind and reap the benefits of healing. Know throughout this process, your choice to embark upon this part of your life's journey is not meant to be an easy one, but it is one in which you are not alone, ever. I am there in spirit, cheering you on the entire way. I know this is right for you, and I believe in you.

2. **START VISUALIZING YOUR DREAMS AND ASPIRATIONS.** Start seeing in your mind's eye what you want to change. Where you want to travel to. What car you want to drive. What goal you want to achieve. See it to be it.

3. **LIVE YOUR BEST LIFE.** When you complete your shadow work, look back for a moment. See where you were before, see where you are now. See all the growth and changes and benefits for your life that you have come to embody along the way. Now,

celebrate yourself! Celebrate your accomplishments and achievements! Celebrate the things that fell away from you because when they did, you became stronger, smarter, more resilient, and more loving. You became more yourself. No one can take these accomplishments and growth from you. You have surpassed all prior ways of being, you have changed yourself for the better, and your life is about to shift to reflect the richness and abundance you found within yourself. This is an auspicious and glorious time in your life. Cry in relief. Cry in joy. Go back out and declare your new Self to the world once more. You are who you are meant to be, you always have been. I am proud of you! You should be proud of yourself.

Epilogue
You Can,
You Are,
You Will

In the summer of 2020, my daughter, my middle child was struggling with her own inner demons. She was struggling with continually feeling as though she was "not enough." With an abusive father and stepmother, she was struggling with the feeling they would never truly see nor embrace who she was. Every argument they would have, she would spiral down a deep pit of depression, barely able to hold on from one week to another for her therapy sessions.

David and I were perpetually crippled with fear. We had her on a continual suicide watch. Feeling as though we could not have both parents out of the house for any duration of time, worried about whether she was going to survive through the night if one of us were not watching out for any tell tale signs that she was dipping too low once more.

It was in those darkest of days, I found the mantra that she would paint on her door in large, bold letters, reminding her everyday of the strength she held within her own heart and mind: You Can, You Are, You Will.

You Can make it through this.

You Are strong enough to survive this.

You Will be stronger when you get to the other side.

You Can, You Are, You Will.

I give these words to you now. Know that no matter what curveballs life throws your way, you can survive anything and everything. You are stronger than you think you are, stronger than you think you know. You will survive every hardship and obstacle that comes your way. You were made for the trials and tribulations in your life.

You were also made for abundant joy and happiness. You were made for this world, for this life, and made to be all you have always dreamt of being. Now is the time for you to go out into the world, taking with you a sense of closure from the whatifs that dance around in your head, silencing the little liar of anxiety within your mind, and living your best life. Live as though you have every possible dream come true just on the horizon of your life. Because you do.

Acknowledgements

From the bottom of my heart I want to thank my family first for being patient with me as I spent long days working on this book. I want to thank my kids and especially David for sitting down and reading this book, for editing when I wasn't able to see the things I missed, and for discussing each of the chapters and steps with me when I felt as though I needed another set of eyes and another mind.

I also want to thank Sue, my beautiful editor, who is always so eager and consistent with reading my books, finding where my commas are missing, and collaborating with me on content matter.

To Amanda, our friendship blossomed in such a beautiful, spiritually mystical manner. I have few words to truly explain just what your friendship has brought into my life. The insights, the camaraderie, and the companionship, still blossoming into something greater, has changed me from my mind to my heart and deep into my soul. Spirit and the Johns definitely brought us together because we are meant to be soul sisters, seeding the light together in this life, and I for one am eager and anxious to see what we can accomplish together.

David, my love. We have struggled, we have warred with ourselves and with each other. We have overcome ex's, issues, discord, and silence. We have found our way back to each other, time after time and we have grown stronger with each joining of our life paths. Thank you for loving all of me, darknesses and light. Thank you for loving my children as your own, for adopting our daughter, for being the hardworking man you are, and for fighting for me when I struggled to fight for myself.

Finally, to all of my friends, family, the Hay House Writer's Community, and my author platform followers, none of the successes I have in my journey as an author would be possible if it were not for your love, support, dedication, and the reading of my writing that you do. Many of you have seen me struggle through my life, have seen me sick, on the brink of death, and have watched me rally, rise, and become who I am today. There is not enough gratitude in the world that would feel adequate for the support you give to me on this journey.

Thank you! Thank you! Thank you!

Chemistry with Kismet: Journeying into the Self to Heal the Mind

Far too easily could my story be misconstrued as one of sorrow and pain if gazing upon it no deeper than surface level. Look to the light, the hope, the love. This is a story of people, famous and mundane alike, whose words, songs, actions, and inactions have impacted my life. This is a story of the pervasive nature of having a life's purpose, and the journey to discover it. This is a story of strength, resilience, perseverance, and the chemistry with kismet bringing me to, or bringing to me, all I required to rise up become

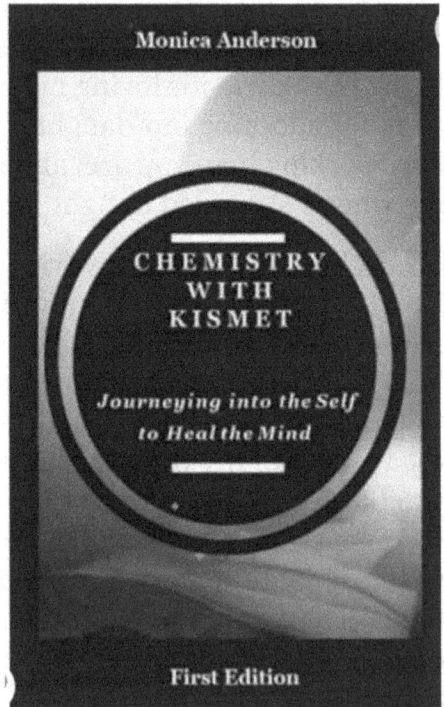

Monica Anderson

CHEMISTRY WITH KISMET

Journeying into the Self to Heal the Mind

First Edition

myself, love myself, and use my once silenced voice for all those still unheard. Available in paperback and ebook on Amazon.com

www.ingramcontent.com/pod-product-compliance
Lightning Source LLC
Chambersburg PA
CBHW061823040426

42447CB00012B/2795